Old Wooden Buildings

Old Wooden Buildings

Donovan Clemson

hancock

house

Copyright © 1978   Donovan Clemson
ISBN 0-919654-90-8

Library of Congress Cataloging in Publication
Data

Clemson, Donovan.
  Old wooden buildings.

  Bibliography: p.
  1. Buildings, Wooden — British Columbia.
2. Architecture — British Columbia — Guide-
books. I. Title.
NA746.B8C55   971.1   77-27836
ISBN 0-919654-90-8

Published simultaneously in Canada and the United States by
Hancock House Publishers

Hancock House Publishers Ltd.

3215 Island View Road
SAANICHTON, B.C. V0S 1M0

Hancock House Publishers Inc.

12008 1st Avenue South
SEATTLE, WA. 98168

Contents

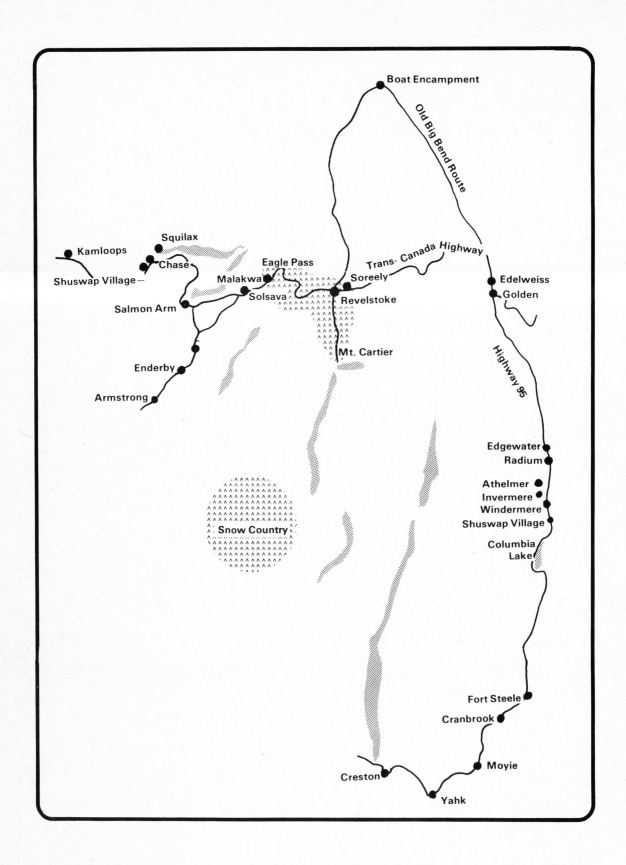

Two Shuswaps

I was farming when this photographic collection of landmarks was commenced, and also contributing articles and photographs to publications with rural circulation, and this sideline led me to explore not only my own neighborhood but as much of the interior as I could without neglecting my farm operations.

There were also excursions prompted by curiosity, and picnics, many picnics, for our family was devoted to this kind of activity. I rarely returned to the farm without some additions to my file of negatives and many of these were of what I regarded at the time as unsaleable material taken with the sole excuse that I liked the subject.Fortunately for this collection I was not influenced by the opinion of a free-lance photographer friend who used to say, "Nice picture, but what would you do with it?" His files contained only saleable stuff, and he was remarkably successful at his profession. But he had no farm to fall back on if sales declined. He couldn't afford the luxury of taking pictures just to please himself.

Ever since the time when my photographs began selling to publications I have regarded the farm as a place of refuge, a haven to which I could retire when editorial response was negative but it was much more than this. It was a little kingdom of which I was the boss, organized to provide me with food, shelter, security, and, most important of all, independence. As long as I paid the taxes I was free to come and go as I pleased, to take advantage of favorable weather conditions to make photographic excursions and enjoy life in general. "What a day for a picnic!" was a common exclamation in our home, to be followed generally by a flurry of activity - the making of

Early Catholic church at O'Keefe's near Vernon. 1966. St. Anne's was built in 1886 in open ranching country near the head of Okanagan Lake and is reputed to be the oldest Catholic church in the area.

sandwiches, the filling of flasks of tea, the hurrying up of the remaining morning chores. Then with the kids off to school, the cows in the pasture and the chickens supplied with feed and water for the day, my wife Doris and I and our excited dogs would climb into the pickup and head for the country roads in whichever direction fancy led. Sometimes indeed the demands of the farm forced upon us some passengers in the form of pet lambs whose feeding schedule called for frequent bottles. We carried them in a crate and I believe they enjoyed each trip and picnic as much as we and our two cocker spaniels.

These day trips rarely took us more than a hundred miles from home but they provided a welcome change of scene as we passed from farming to ranching country where in the more open landscape the buildings of the pioneer settlers stood out as prominent landmarks visible from afar. Of these by far the most striking were the tall churches of the native villages which were scattered through the interior. The pattern used to be pretty constant: A cluster of log houses of modest dimensions with a handsome frame church occupying a place of prominence. Nearly always the church would be well-maintained, making a strange contrast with the rest of the village whose log dwellings were of course not subject to periodic painting like the dressed siding of the churches. Often the repainting of the church ended part way up the steeple, the baffled villagers apparently not having devised a scaffolding for such heights. And many of the native churches were tall. Through the Thompson, Nicola, Cariboo and Skeena areas the survivors of these interesting and picturesque old buildings gracefully complement the natural features of the interior landscape.

But change has come to the villages. Frame houses are replacing the old log homes and some of the tall churches have been lost by fire and replaced by squat, low structures with token spires six feet high. In such situations the church is no longer recognized as part of the scenery and the village has lost its character. What does it matter? says the villager. The new church is comfortable, and it's certainly easier to paint. But to me it matters very much. Some well-remembered landmarks have disappeared and will not be replaced. Change which is inevitable offers us hydro poles and wires to decorate our landscapes with, and slick, straight highways which can never mellow enough to harmonize with the scenery.

In Shuswap Village in the Upper Columbia Valley south of Golden, 1958. Far from the Shuswap Country this church marks the site of a settlement established by migrating Shuswaps led by Kinbasket, a North Thompson chief about 1840.

In Squilax Village, Shuswap country, 1964. Catholic Church of St. Peter and St. Paul occupies a flat by Little River, a short stream connecting Shuswap and Little Shuswap Lakes.

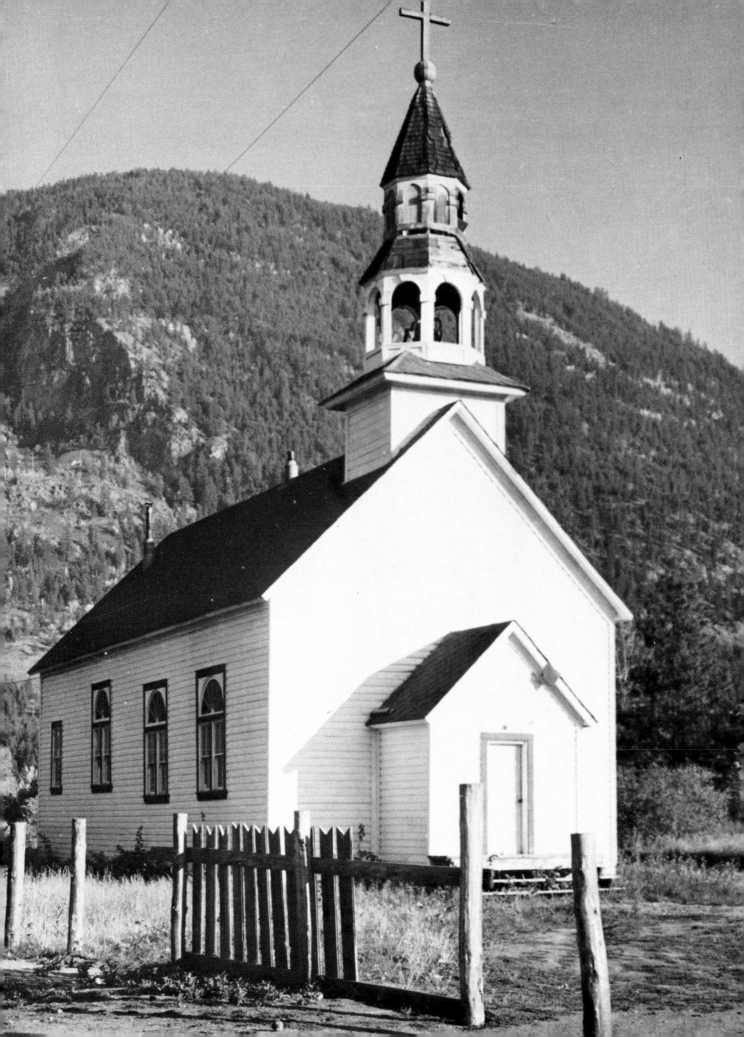

Catholic church in native village at Enderby, 1963. St. Mary's was built about 1890 and later moved to its present location from the original site in open country.

A Falkland church in Salmon River Valley, 1960. Christ Church, Anglican, sits at the roadside on Highway 97.

• *Note the difference between the steeples of the two churches.*

Since I first started collecting these old landmarks several of the village churches have disappeared. At Lillooet, Bridge River, Fountain and Shuswap the scenery has been impaired by the loss of attractive churches. Shuswap church - alas my favorite - stood on the north bank of the South Thompson River about one and a half hour's drive from the farm and being so close it became the subject of many photographs at all seasons. Shuswap village actually straddles the river but most of the houses snuggled up to the church on the north bank. It was a tall graceful church set in a pleasant landscape blessed with the interesting variations of seasonal change. Spring turned the bare background hills yellow with the massed blooms of Balsam Root, the wild sunflower of the interior. In summer the brimming river reflected the charming scene in its glassy surface while winter isolated the tableau of church and homes in an expanse of white.

Into this idyllic scene came the ubiquitous tentacles of hydro bringing the blessings of light, running water, electric can-openers and T.V. to the inhabitants. Two huge poles supporting the river span were planted in front of the church and painted red and white to provide a gaudy frame for the edifice. The effect was striking if not artistic but the beautiful old church did not long survive the indignity inflicted upon it. In 1974 it burned down leaving the painted poles in sole possession of the site.

Post office and store at Yahk, 1960.

12

Shuswap Village church, 1971. Decorative poles courtesy B.C. Hydro. Built in 1894, it was an interesting South Thompson landmark until destroyed by fire in 1974.

St. Michael's was eighty years old almost to the day when a November 4th fire destroyed it. Consecrated November 5th, 1894 it became a familiar landmark to travelers on the Trans-Canada Highway which passes on the other side of the river. Since the loss of the church the village has declined as a local "sight." All the houses are

*Farm house near Armstrong, 1958.
Type of house popular in the early
1900's.*

now frame and more livable, certainly, than the small log homes of former times, and it is true the church had not been used regularly for service in later years as modern transportation has made it so easy for adherents to worship in the larger centers. Chase village with its large church is only five miles away. But the old village appealed to me in a way a modern settlement never can, especially if its principal feature is a pair of brightly painted power poles. Many times I passed through the old village on our frequent day excursions, for the Thompson Valley is one of our favorite haunts. There were outings to hunt for arrowheads and other artifacts which are to be found on the river bars at periods of low water, and special trips to see the spring wildflowers which are quite exceptional in the region. There were pauses in the village to photograph and visit friends, and always to admire the church. Recurring memories bring back incidents of those past times. I remember naked children splashing in the flood water on the grassy river bank. I remember the little cemetery on the hill and my friend,

Mrs. Isaac Willard, kneeling by her son's fresh grave after he was drowned while swimming the river.

Far away, in the Columbia Lakes country, there is another village called Shuswap. Its roadside church is seen by travelers on the Golden-Cranbrook road in the vicinity of Windermere, and it owes its origin to a band of Shuswaps that migrated to the region about the year 1840. James Teit, the historian of the Shuswap, relates in a memoir of The American Museum of Natural History, 1908, how Kinbasket, a North Thompson chief, led sixty followers to the new location where they established themselves in the country of the Kootenays. The band migrated down the Canoe River to the Big Bend where it joined the Columbia thence upstream to the lakes country. Teit says they succeeded in maintaining their hold in the new country by forming an alliance with the Stony

Carpenter's delight, a farm house near Armstrong, North Okanagan Valley dating from the early years of the century.

Indians of the Rocky Mountains who were in the habit of coming to the Kootenay country to fish for salmon.

I was intrigued and gratified when coming upon Shuswap's pretty church so far from the real Shuswap country. We were on a journey of exploration of several days duration at the time, having driven over the old Big Bend road which proved singularly lacking in interesting landmarks. True, there was Old Woodenhead, a large carved stump at Boat Encampment, on a high bank to which many tourists had beaten a path, but it was isolated by many miles of dense, continuous timber each way.

At Boat Encampment on the Old Big Bend Road, 1960. The road opened in 1940, followed the Columbia Valley from Golden to Revelstoke through continuous forest. Old Wooden Head, a carved stump about half way along the route, was one of the few landmarks to look for.

Stores at Golden, 1960. Originally Golden City, a mining settlement, but actually brought to life by the building of the C.P.R. through the mountains.

Front of guide's house, Edelweiss Village, Golden, 1960. Built by C.P.R. to accommodate Swiss guides when climbing in the Selkirks was popular at the turn of the century.

The Upper Columbia Valley was different though. There was the little village of Edelweiss perched on the mountainside overlooking Golden, a reminder of the mountaineering days when the Selkirk peaks attracted many climbers from overseas. The five Swiss-type houses were built by Canadian Pacific Railway in 1911 and 1912 to house guides and their families. Swiss guides were introduced in 1899 when climbing in the Selkirks became very popular. They were stationed at Glacier where they were quite at home among the peaks and glaciers but they missed the picturesque houses they had been used to in their native land. To keep them contented and ease the pangs of homesickness the C.P.R. undertook to build them a village in the style of those in their homeland. But climbing eventually tapered off, the guides departed, and in 1960 the pretty houses were in private hands.

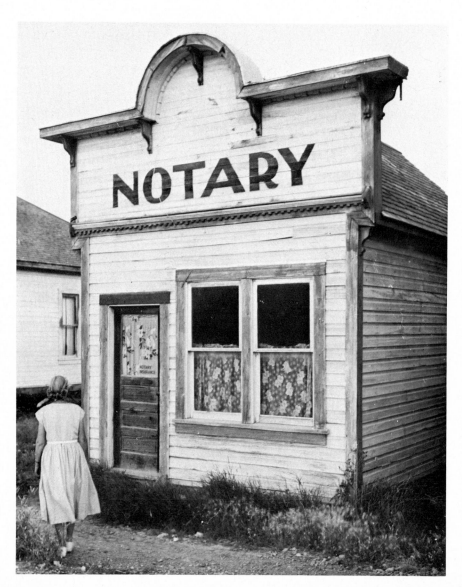

Office building at Athelmer in the Upper Columbia Valley, 1962.

We were in older country now, with a history going back to David Thompson's wanderings in the early nineteenth century. There were small communities with fascinating old buildings in varying stages of decay, and at Invermere on a sandhill overlooking Windermere Lake a memorial to the great traveler, an enormous log building, erected in the nineteen-twenties, showed the results of weathering and neglect.

Anglican church at Edgewater, an Upper Columbia community, 1960.

It appeared that the inhabitants of this interesting old valley had a craze for collecting burl-stricken trees, debarking them and using them for gate posts or planting them to stand like totem poles in their gardens. I saw a splendid specimen in a garden at Golden and asked if I could photograph it. The owner, a priest, donned his habit and posed beside his specimen. Farther south at Radium the burl-totems grew larger and taller. Outside a store I saw one that was at least eighteen feet tall furnished with burls from top to bottom. It was evident there was keen competition among the burl-fanciers who were trying to outdo each other. I knew the national parks people were keen to procure burl trees for their signs and had many interesting specimens to exhibit but their best efforts were dwarfed by the Radium burls.

I discovered an industrious rancher nearby who had plans to excel even the monster burls on view at Radium. Jim Thompson of Canyon Ranch was busy forking hay to some cattle but he paused to discuss with enthusiasm his latest acquisition in the way of burls. The huge specimen lay in his yard, a log over twenty feet long which was a complete series of burls, some of which were four feet in diameter. "Did you have to go far for this fellow," I asked. "Not far," Jim replied, "about fifty miles, I reckon. It was growing up Horse Thief Creek. My brother found it while prospecting. We took the jeep in - didn't have to cut more than half a mile of road to get at it. There's another one there," he added, thoughtfully, and he described a large spruce - burls all the way up, large at the bottom, reducing in size towards the top, like a Chinese pagoda. Jim intended to get this one also and make an imposing entrance to his ranch. I never did get to see the finished work but I'm sure it must have made a burl landmark that will not be easily surpassed.

Burl specimen at Radium, Upper Columbia Valley.

This Columbia trip took us eventually to Cranbrook where we hunted up the big old waterwheel of Perry Creek. Surely no landmark was more effectively hidden away than this! Once discovered it loomed high in a timbered creek bottom, the chief of a cluster of old relics of a former gold-mining operation and a silent witness to the spirit and enterprise of the pioneer miners. It was used to provide power for dewatering a mine but the operation was not profitable. Local historians feared their big wheel was being missed by tourists so it was dragged out of the bush and installed at nearby Fort Steele where, sitting beside the highway, it cannot be overlooked. Fort Steele itself, the original Mounted Police post in British Columbia, has been bisected by the new highway and rearranged to accommodate the many tourists that visit it.

Water wheel on old mining operation at Perry Creek near Cranbrook, 1963. The wheel has since been removed to Fort Steele. Gold was first discovered at Perry Creek in 1867 but there was sporadic mining activity until the nineteen thirties.

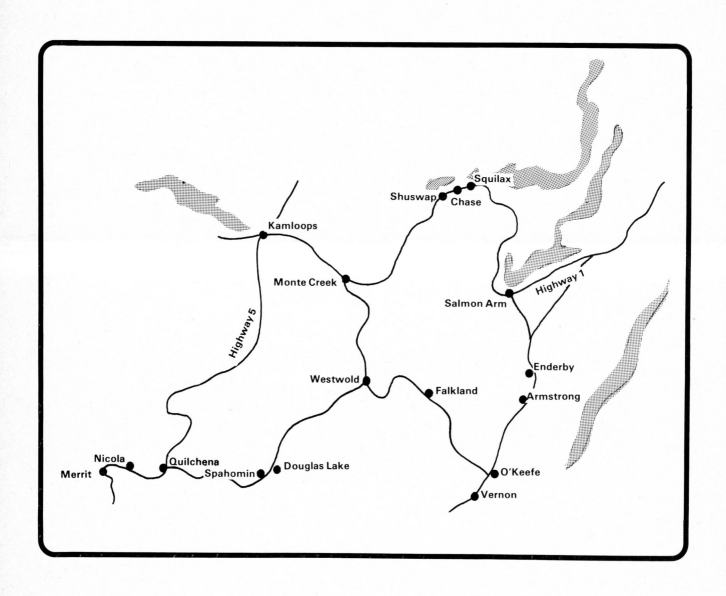

Ranching Country.

Because we were dry-farmers we had the time to make frequent trips in the interior. Our North Okanagan farm was in an area of moderate precipitation - twelve to eighteen inches - which was usually sufficient to grow successfully a great variety of crops. Besides the field crops, we grew for our own use apples, pears, plums, cherries, raspberries, grapes, currants and watermelons, and all the vegetables we required. We never envied the irrigation farmer with his endless round of work contending with heavy and continuous production which keeps him busy through the summer, particularly in the months of July and August. These were actually our slackest months. We endeavored to put up our hay in early June and when that was safely in the barn we looked forward to a more or less leisurely period as

Pasture gate, Douglas Lake Ranch. The road from Westwold to the Nicola Country crosses the fenced pastures of the huge Douglas Lake Ranch and the motorist is expected to open and close the gates when pastures are in use. Large pitchy pine posts have long life in the ground.

summer advanced. Depending on the rain we received, a second crop of alfalfa would be shaping up, the grain growing and maturing, and the potato fields, after the final cultivation, needing little attention until harvest time. We could leave the farm for a week at a time without anything suffering. Of course there were always jobs we could be doing but we turned a blind eye to these if they threatened to impede our explorations of the back country.

Our many trips always produced revenue. Pictures of other farmers and ranchers at work found a market with farm publications. For this reason we generally sallied forth on weekdays when nearly everyone else was at work. And the file of landmark negatives grew steadily larger. I usually did my darkroom work evenings after the farm operations for the day had been accomplished, and frequently worked till 10 p.m. processing film and making prints in the little darkroom I had built at one end of our large farm kitchen.

Some of our earliest trips led us into the Nicola country and the grassy domain of the Douglas Lake Ranch where the almost treeless landscape offered such a striking contrast to the wooded mountains of our own locality. We loved the narrow dirt road that rambled over the spacious terrain, passing a few clusters of ranch buildings and the odd log fence snaking over the treeless

Barn at Douglas Lake Ranch, 1959. A low-pitched roof suited to the light snowfall of the interior drybelt valleys.

Photo on preceding page
←

*Old Catholic church at Spahomin Village
near Douglas Lake, 1970. Built in 1888 the
old church stands apart from the village in
a setting of open grassy hills.*

hills. Here the voluptuous earth revealed itself in swelling ridges that continued mile after mile until cresting in a dark line of timber on the far horizon. "Undulating bunch grass country," it is designated on an old map - 1884 - of British Columbia, and the Douglas Lake grasslands still fit that description while other areas in the interior so described have been degraded by the invasion of sagebrush.

The village of Spahomin sits in this bare landscape and in a distant view appears in miniature, a cluster of toy houses and a toy church. Like most of the native churches it has a tall bell tower and is of course the most prominent building in the village. Spahomin has a new church now, a low building in the modern style, situated at the opposite end of the settlement, and the old church sits alone and isolated from the village which, with its new additions, seems to be drifting away from it. An informant in the village told me that it was built in 1888.

*Spahomin church, Douglas Lake country, 1969. It sits in a
parched landscape of treeless hills.*

Photo on preceding page

Stacks of baled hay for winter stock feed
are a common sight in ranching country.
This scene is at Westwold on the side road
leading to Douglas Lake.

We nearly always came into the Nicola country over
the Douglas Lake grasslands by means of the little old
road that starts from Westwold on the Vernon-Kamloops
highway. It is really one of those short-cuts that use up so
much more time than the longer way round on the
highway but it appealed to us because it meandered
through country that changes very little with the years. It
has always been cattle country to the rancher and will
probably maintain its character for many years to come,
a comforting thought in these times of rapid change. This
road, after leaving Spahomin, emerges on Highway 5 -
Princeton-Kamloops - at the native village of Quilchena, a
location well-marked by the church at the junction of the
roads.

Typical dry-belt scenery predominates through the
valley of the Nicola. The yellow pine is at home, sparingly
dotting the open hillsides with solitary trees, often
crooked and windblown. There are craggy rock outcrops
and in deep hollows small lakes. Settlement is sparse and
for that reason the local landmarks are prominent. One of
the most striking, the old Quilchena Hotel, has exhibited
its imposing three-story facade beside the Merritt-
Kamloops road for many years, a white elephant, doomed
from the start by early prohibition laws, unoccupied
except by numerous swallows who attach their mud nests
to the eaves. In late years the old building has been used
in summer as a ranch guest house so life is beginning to
stir in the long-empty rooms.

A Nicola Valley landmark, the old Quilchena Hotel beside the Merrit to Kamloops road. Its early carreer was checked
by prohibition laws and for years it
remained empty but is now used in
summer as a ranch guest house. It was
built in 1908.

Another valley landmark for many years was the big barn of Nicola Stock Farms at Nicola but unfortunately it suffered the fate of many other wooden buildings of the interior and burned several years ago. It was a splendid example of a ranch barn of the horse-power period with a loft designed for the storage of large quantities of loose hay.

I well remember that time, having worked on interior ranches in the late nineteen-twenties before the mechanical revolution had depopulated the bunkhouses and rendered the pitchfork almost as obsolete as the flail.

Barn of Nicola Stock Farms, 1962. This was a well-known landmark on Highway 5 where it passed through Nicola until it was destroyed by fire.

Then horses and men were relied on for putting up the annual hay crop and feeding it out again in winter. The mechanical aids available at the time still required the services of the horse and the man with the pitchfork. They lightened the labor of the latter but did not displace him. Sweeps, hay-loaders and derricks speeded up the operation of hay-making and made it possible to build large stacks, while barn lofts were filled by means of specially designed hoisting apparatus worked by horse power. Some relics of the period may still be seen in ranching country in the Nicola, Cariboo and Chilcotin districts where large crews were employed at haying time. Most conspicuous are the old stacking derricks that were built and assembled on the ranch using timber from the adjoining bush. They were designed to hoist a slingload of hay from a sloop or wagon and swing it on to a stack where a couple of hands with pitchforks would quickly spread it.

Time is gradually thinning out the big barns and the relics but the old-time haying scene has completely vanished. Gone are the thousands of hay cocks that used to cover the meadows, the many teams hauling sloops and wagons, and the field pitchers loading them; and gone is the derrick team at the busy center of the picture constantly swinging loads to the stack from the steady parade that came in from the field. All this has been replaced by one man, or a girl, on a tractor pulling a pickup baler, thump, thump, thump, dropping rectangular bales evenly spaced round and round the meadow in reducing laps; and a later operation employing several hands when the bales are collected and stacked by means of a motor-driven elevator. These stacks of baled hay have introduced a new pattern into the ranching landscape, and the big barns with stalls for teams of horses and loft accommodation for many tons of loose hay are no longer considered essential to ranch operations.

A very different type of barn which has achieved the status of a local landmark is encountered in the Columbia Valley in the vicinity of Revelstoke at no great distance from the dry ranges of the Nicola but unlike that region in climate and topography.

House at Nicola, 1962. A landmark on the Merritt Kamloops Road, Highway 5.

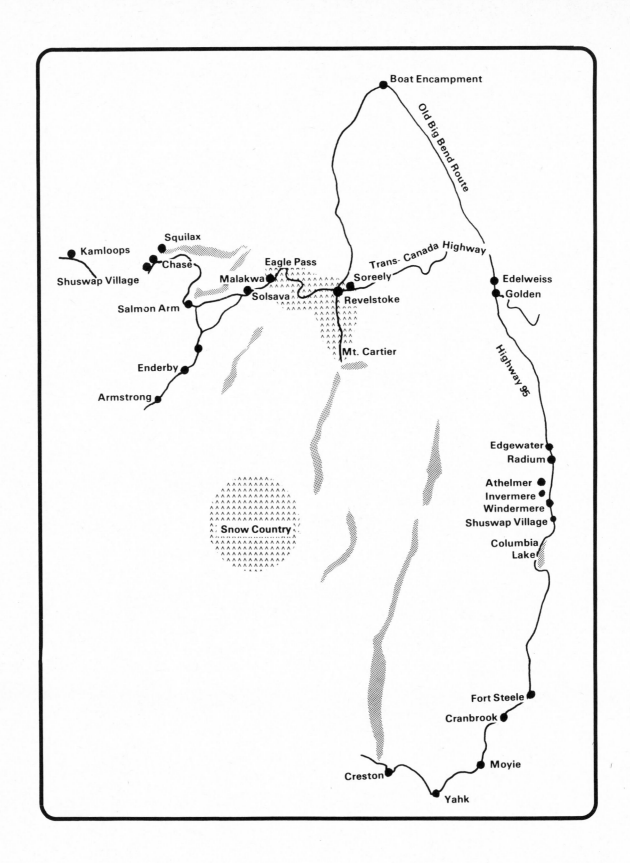

In the Big Snow Country.

Revelstoke was about eighty miles east of our farm, further than the Nicola which lay fifty miles in the opposite direction, but though the combined distance was not great the two regions represented extremes in interior scenery due to the great difference in precipitation. Not only was the scenery influenced by the local climatic conditions which decided the nakedness of the hills in one area and the dense forest in the other. The farmers and ranchers themselves, with their barns, corrals and fence patterns, added details to the landscape which were sometimes peculiar to their own locality. Such was the case in the Revelstoke area which we visited frequently on day trips between farm chores. There we found the ultimate in barn roof design - a roof built to shed rather than support the enormous weight of snow which in a normal winter falls on the district.

Driving through Eagle Valley from Sicamous on we had noticed the barn roofs getting steeper as we progressed. At Malakwa the hip roof that is so popular in large barns had been modified to provide a very narrow upper segment - the part that carries the weight of snow - while the lower section was long and steep enough to allow the snow to slide off. These steepening roofs indicated increasing snowfall as we approached the Selkirks. When within the shadow of these mountains in the vicinity of Revelstoke we discovered barns that were actually all roof, triangular in shape and towering high, steep pinnacles that introduced an original detail into the farming scene.

Barn in Columbia Valley, south of Revelstoke, 1956. The ultimate in Columbia Valley barn roof design. This building is on a small farm south of Revelstoke. The narrow loft probably holds barely enough hay to winter the family cow.

Columbia barn in winter. A winter view of the building on opposite page showing the small barn bravely resisting the deluge of snow usual in the vicinity of the Selkirk Mountains.

We found these remarkable barns in the Illecillewaet Valley and in the agricultural district south of the town under the shadow of Mt. Cartier where, we were assured by residents, the snowfall is indeed heavy. The construction is simple if not primitive, for when viewed from the front the term wigwam seems actually more appropriate than barn. The long straight poles used for rafters are products of the local forest which is dense and tall and also supplies the cedar for the hand-made shakes that cover the building. The largest barn we saw was about thirty-six feet wide at the base and more than forty feet in height; it had the capacity for a considerable quantity of hay. The rafters, which of course are about the only timbers used in the building, are set in the ground four to six feet apart to form a very strong frame, then horizontal sheathing is laid on to which the shakes are attached. Despite the size of the poles used for rafters - eight inches or more on the butt - we saw one barn where these timbers were not equal to the strain put upon them, several of the rafters being sprung near the base by the enormous quantity of snow accumulating against the building.

Barn at Greely, Illecillewaet, 1958. A few miles out of Revelstoke near the Rogers Pass Road, this is probably the largest of the Columbia Valley steep-roofed barns with a capacity for storing a large quantity of hay.

United church, at Malakwa in the Eagle Valley, 1964. The metal roof is a common feature of buildings in this area with its ability to shed snow.

The unique barns were not the only attractions of the region for us. The mountains themselves were sufficient to lure us back time after time, for they were high and steep, crowned with permanent snow and ice, with deep valleys between. There were roadside waterfalls dropping down from mountainsides rich with devil's club and maidenhair fern. Against this pristine background the works of the settlers posed in miniature - log houses, barns, saunas, rail fences and woodpiles. But there were fields too that offered wider foregrounds to the mountain scenery. At Solsqua in Eagle Valley farmers of Finnish origin adopted the methods of their homeland to cure hay in their narrow vale where often high moisture conditions hindered the process. The hay was cured off the ground on stakes in the form of small narrow stacks which dotted the fields in June and July. It formed a pattern new to us which we never encountered elsewhere but it was strictly a scene from the pitchfork era and did not survive the invasion of modern hay-making machinery.

Hayfield at Solsqua in the Eagle Valley, 1958. Once an annual sight from Highway 1 approaching Eagle Pass, the old hand method has been eliminated by modern haymaking equipment.

Steep roofed barn at Malakwa, Eagle Valley, 1965. A sturdy building designed to cope with the heavy snowfall of the district which increases as Highway 1 approaches Revelstoke and Rogers Pass.

South of Revelstoke most of the old landmarks familiar to travelers disappeared when the building of Arrow Dam caused the inundation of the shoreline of the Arrow Lakes and the river valley which fed them. The route to the Kootenay with its river and lake ferries and waterside hotels ceased to exist. The community of Arrowhead, long time steamboat and railroad terminus, was erased though many of the buildings including a little church were well above the flood level. The place was isolated by the flood water, however, and now can be reached only by boat.

Arrowhead church, 1964. Destroyed with rest of community after completion of Arrowhead Dam. Used by several denominations this little church stood high above most of the old settlement.

Perhaps the most notable of the old landmarks on this route was the hotel at St. Leon, the site of some hot springs near the shore of Upper Arrow Lake about half way between old Arrowhead and Nakusp. It was really an astonishing sight to the lake traveler of old as the steamboat or ferry passed the little cove on which it was situated. There was a beach of pure sand and a small clearing, and there sat the huge building, its three-storied front facing the lake - beyond and on either side nothing but forest and mountain.

St. Leon was built at great cost early in the century by a mining man who, it is said, made a fortune in the Slocan mines. His idea was to utilize the water of the hot springs which were a couple of miles back up the mountain and supposed to possess curative qualities. The venture apparently was not successful and for many years the hotel remained untenanted. In the late nineteen-forties a new owner acquired the building and some business subsequently ensued but by the time Arrow Dam was nearing completion it was again unoccupied. Shortly before the rising water invaded the site the old landmark was destroyed by fire of mysterious origin.

St. Leon Hotel, early Arrow Lakes landmark, 1965. Situated on Upper Arrow Lake about half way between Arrow Head and Nakusp it was once a popular resort for holiday makers. Built early in the century, it was destroyed by fire shortly before rising water from the Arrow Dam flooded the site.

Store at Rosebery, Slocan Lake, 1959. Slocan a mining district in the Kootenays which reached its peak of activity in the early nineteen-hundreds. Many of the buildings are in the style of those early days.

Stores at Kaslo, 1959.

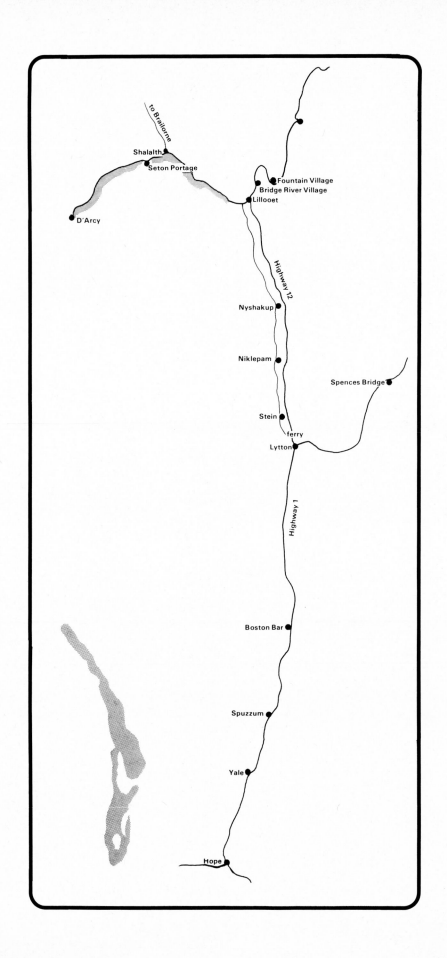

to Brailorne

Shalalth
Seton Portage

D'Arcy

Fountain Village
Bridge River Village
Lillooet

Highway 12

Nyshakup

Niklepam

Spences Bridge

Stein
ferry
Lytton

Highway 1

Boston Bar

Spuzzum

Yale

Hope

Fraser Canyon Landmarks.

While fire has been responsible for the removal of many of the old interior landmarks it is only one of the agents constantly at work modifying the scenery. Changing fashions in agriculture and mechanical developments have had a marked effect on the rural landscape. And the railroad scene, generally regarded as a fairly permanent feature, has lost a familiar detail since the diesel locomotive took over from the steamer. The water tower has vanished from its trackside location. Up till 1958 when I photographed the last steam locomotive on the Okanagan branch line, the water tower and the steam locomotive taking on water were essential details of railroading but by 1963 the water tower had become a curiosity. I photographed one at Shuswap on the C.P.R. main line in that year but that is the last I have seen.

Once a common sight along railroads, water towers are no longer to be seen. This one was at Shuswap on C.P.R. main line, 1963.

Deep in the Fraser Canyon is the little Catholic church at Yale, 1957. Dwarfed by the high rocks of the canyon this little church occupies a small bench a short distance from the village.

The passing of the water tower was probably the least remarkable of the modern changes in the rural landscape. Painted with the traditional dull C.P.R. red that pretty well camouflaged it from the roving eye of the passing traveler, it was such a homely object that its decease must have gone largely unnoticed. Other old landmarks have been isolated or by-passed by highway improvements and are now known only to frequenters of side-roads and by-ways; and road construction itself with its greater demands on wayside space has eliminated buildings, fences, rocks and trees that served as milestones to the leisurely travelers of former times.

Nowhere is this trend more evident than in the lower Fraser Canyon which has been an important transportation route since the eighteen-sixties when the Cariboo Wagon Road was built to give the province its first road into the interior. Later the railroad came and construction eliminated parts of the old road which was rendered unusable. But in the nineteen-twenties demands for a road connection with the interior resulted in the repair and re-opening of the old route for summer use. A new bridge was built on the site of the original Fraser crossing established over a century ago in the gorge a few miles upstream from Spuzzum. The Alexandra Bridge was a notable landmark for the traveler of the period and remained so until 1963 when the new high-level bridge by-passed it together with a stretch of canyon road considered inadequate for modern traffic.

The old Alexandra Bridge in the Fraser Canyon, 1961. It spans a narrow stretch of the canyon on the site of the original bridge which was built in 1863.

Although our introduction to the canyon route came as late as 1952 it was still an adventure to drive it, for, with the exception of a few miles of wide new highway south of Lytton, the road was in rather a primitive state. Nearly all of it was narrow and of course crooked. There were deep incursions where one drove for many miles up side valleys to detour some precipitous gorge that barred the direct way; and there were narrow stretches where the track, edging around some vertical cliff, allowed no room to pass another vehicle. But it was a leisurely road, full of interest and opportunities for observation. I photographed little churches at Inkasap, Spuzzum, Yale, and old Indian cemeteries clinging to the steep canyon sides. There were scenic shots too, to be had at almost every roadside halt, for Hydro's transmission lines had not yet appeared in the canyon. Our first view of the Alexandra Bridge was spectacular. We had stopped for the umpteenth time to look at the view, and saw very far below what appeared to be a slender thread spanning the river. It was the bridge, almost lost in the immensity of the canyon, and so far below that we wondered how we would accomplish the descent.

But the thrills that once accompanied the canyon trip are no longer to be had. A previous day's driving is now accomplished in a few hours at highway speeds over a straightened road; deep gorges are spanned by high steel bridges, and cliff-hanging stretches by-passed by tunnels bored through the rock. The old landmarks that remain are no longer prominent objects to the motorist hurrying by.

A different atmosphere is sensed in the canyon north of Lytton where Trans-Canada Highway leaves it to follow the Thompson gorge to Kamloops. The drone of traffic disappears with the highway into the Thompson's spectacular canyon, leaving the Fraser's course strangely quiet. Apart from Hydro's far-reaching pylons and wires the canyon scene between Lytton and Williams Lake has changed little over the last century. It is still mostly wild land, far too rough and steep for agriculture to gain more than a precarious foothold on the small isolated benches which show as tiny green patches in the immense landscape of rock and mountain. The occasional picturesque church bespeaks a sparse native population, not established in villages as in the plateau country but scattered,

In a deserted village, Bridge River, 1969. Situated on a bench at the junction of Fraser and Bridge River it was once a populous native community as indicated by the old cemetery but has been deserted for many years.

Holy Redeemer Church, native village, Lillooet 1958. Destroyed with the whole village in 1971 when a forest fire swept in off the mountain.

Native cemetery with view of the Fraser, Lytton, 1952.

hidden and tucked away in tiny hollows and recesses of the great canyon. Such isolated churches are found on the west side of the river at Stein and Nicklepam and Nyshakup where a road of sorts, not long upgraded from a trail, permits the motorist to traverse the rugged forty miles between Lytton Ferry and Lillooet.

The Lillooet country used to possess a number of interesting churches which, in the nineteen-fifties when our trips to that fascinating country began, were to be seen and admired in the villages of Pavilion, Fountain, Bridge River and Lillooet, but of these only the old church at Pavilion remains. Bridge River was already a deserted village when its church burned in 1971 but its situation at the confluence of Bridge River and the Fraser in the midst of the wildest of mountain scenery rendered it one of the most memorable of the canyon sights. Very little of the village survives - a few log buildings and roofless remains amongst the sagebrush which has invaded the site, and a well-stocked cemetery nearby.

In D'Arcy Village at the west end of Anderson Lake on the early gold rush route to the Cariboo creeks.

Photo on preceding page

Old log Catholic church at Lillooet, 1965. At one time covered with siding this old building stands beside the Seton Lake road. It is the last survivor of Lillooet's old churches.

Church of St. Augustine, Nyshakup in the canyon country between Lillooet and Lytton. With no level site available this tiny church stands on a steep hillside high above the Fraser River which occupies the canyon beyond.

Near Lillooet town is a very old native church whose history I have been unable to discover. It stands beside the Seton Lake road set against a typical Lillooet background of steep mountain, its ancient hewn logs and weathered shingles in perfect harmony with the canyon landscape. Even the siding, with which it has at some time been partially covered, has mellowed to match the dusty tints of the surrounding sagebrush. To me this neglected little church in its wonderful setting exudes the essential atmosphere of Lillooet. For Lillooet is old, old, as our brief history goes. By-passed by the rush of progress it rests quietly on its sunny bench, a gold rush town that survived and integrated with the canyon landscape, even to the ancient bridge that spans the turbid Fraser and gives it access to the outside world.

The prevailing peaceful atmosphere is also evident in an adjacent deep valley where slender spires mark the villages of Shalalth and Seton Portage. This is the western pass that admitted the gold rush traffic to Lillooet in the eighteen-sixties and later accommodated the adventurous track of the P.G.E. The valley is occupied by the two lakes, Seton and Anderson, which are separated by a narrow strip of land known as Seton Portage. The scenery is fiord-like and unusually beautiful with high mountains rising steeply from the deep, narrow lakes, and snow peaks seemingly suspended in the sky. In this idyllic picture the little churches of the natives have their place, gently reminding us that it is possible for man and his environment to exist in harmony.

St. Paul's Catholic Church in Shalalth Village, Seton Lake, 1969. With little flat ground available between the steep mountain wall and the deep lake St. Paul's clings to the hillside at the foot of Mission Ridge.

Stein Church in Fraser Canyon, near Lytton, 1973. This small church on its boulder strewn flat stands apart from Stein Village across the river from Lytton and can be reached by ferry.

Lillooet, village church of Holy Redeemer, 1959. In the foreground the leaning frame of an earlier church. The village was destroyed by fire in 1971.

But to the seeker of untarnished rustic beauty there are jarring notes. Like a serpent in the Garden of Eden the daily freight of the British Columbia Railway moves noisily through the lovely valley accompanied by a succession of shrill shrieks, squeals, squeaks and groans as the wheels grind round the numerous curves in the track. Over the tranquil lakes floats this mechanical symphony, assaulting the sensitive ear until cut off by some distant bend. And Hydro's mighty works, pylons set in impossible places, wires swooping from mountain to mountain, however gratifying to the engineer, are most disturbing elements in the scenery.

Although so close to Lillooet this valley is accessible to the motorist only by a long and roundabout route which follows the canyon of Bridge River for many rugged miles, then climbs steeply to the summit of Mission Ridge to make a zig-zag 3000 foot descent to Seton Lake.

In Seton Portage cemetery, 1967. This native burial ground is beautifully situated on a small bench overlooking Anderson Lake and the Narrow Valley which is the route of B.C. Railway into the interior.

This small Fraser Canyon church stands beside the highway at Boston Bar, 1959.

St. Aidan's of Pokhaist Village stands in the sagebrush of the arid Thompson Valley near Spences Bridge, 1960.

Old ranch house, Duck Range, South Thompson Valley, 1965. Near Pritchard on Highway 1. Built in the style in favor in the first two decades of the century.

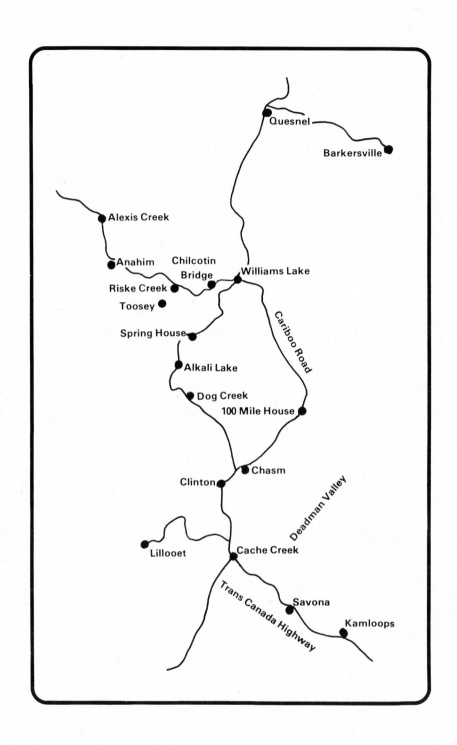

Cariboo Relics.

Half a century ago, when I first saw the Cariboo country, the old road which was built in the eighteen-sixties was pretty much on its original location, and many of the roadside hostelries that became established along the route in the old freighting days were still to be seen. It was a gravel road and as I remember it was frequently in that condition known as washboard which made traveling in the automobiles of the period slow and uncomfortable, conditions which the P.G.E. duplicated in its twice weekly mixed passenger and freight train into the interior. The

Old freight wagon wheels fence a garden at 14 mile on old Cariboo road north of Lillooet, 1955. Fourteen mile was a favorite stopping place for the freight wagons out of Lillooet on the terrific up-hill haul to the top of Pavilion Mountain.

railway then was still regarded as a newcomer to the Cariboo for it had only a few years previously ousted the freight teams from the famous road. Displaced freighting teamsters were to be found on many of the roadside ranches where they entertained the bunk-house crowd with thrilling stories of their exploits and experiences. I heard stories of ox teams and mule teams as well as the many large horse teams that were engaged in the traffic, and of the long, uphill haul from Ashcroft to Clinton in the busy days when as many as one hundred teams would stop at Clinton for the night. At the Mound Ranch near Clinton where I was employed for a time I found ox shoes among other relics in the dirt outside the blacksmith's shop.

Ranchers barn, Deadman Valley. A dry valley occupied by small ranches and a native village trending north from Highway 1 near Savona. In the dry climate hay is stacked in the open and such small barns are used for the accommodation of saddle horses.

Photo on preceding page

By the Cariboo road north of Cache Creek, Catholic church in Bonaparte Village, 1958. The Cariboo road bisects this old village, with the cemetery across from the church showing many ancient inscriptions.

Perhaps ten years had elapsed since motorized freight hauling and the railway had supplanted the teamsters but some of the old road houses were operating still, catering to the daily stage passengers. I remember the roadside stops, the hospitality, the fifty-cent meals on platters. I remember the obliging stage driver stopping to give his passengers time to view the famous chasm north of Clinton which the modern highway by-passes by several miles. At that time the relics of the road, apart from the road houses, were not uncommon. A number of stage coaches were to be seen, some of them repainted and displayed at stopping places, and some of the freight wagons doubtless saw service on neighboring ranches. At Chilco Ranch in the Chilcotin where I worked as a ranch hand in 1928 the cowboys got hold of a discarded stage coach and converted it into a chuck wagon. Unfortunately, when they headed for the range on the fall roundup they entrusted the new outfit, of which they were very proud, to a teamster instead of a cook, an ill-considered move for which they later expressed regret.

In the Chilcotin Valley, church at Anahim Rancherie, 1964. A prominent landmark situated on a bench above the Chilcotin Road, commanding a wide view of the river flats.

Catholic church at Clinton, 1956.

Native church, Deadman Creek Village, 1959. Deadman Valley runs north from Highway 1 near Savona. The well-maintained church is a bright landmark in the dry valley with its red and brown rock exposures.

By the time I was in a position to record the old landmarks on the road many of them had disappeared and the road itself had changed greatly. We rode out the depression on our North Okanagan farm. There were no hardships but we were limited to horse and buggy transportation which confined our explorations to our immediate neighborhood. Eventually we became mechanized with the acquisition of a 1925 Dodge touring car which extended our radius of operations considerably, but it was not until 1950 that we were really enabled to take to the road and travel the interior highways. With the help of our good friends and neighbors, who were always willing to look after our livestock during our absence, we started making trips of more than a day's duration.

In the arid Thompson Valley near Ashcroft, the tiny Indian log church at Ashcroft Manor.

Pavilion cemetery and village on the old Cariboo Road, 1961. From the church the old road, still in use, snaked steeply upward to the summit of the mountain in the background before making an even steeper descent to Kelly Lake.

St. Saviour's Church, Barkerville, 1960. A favourite sight in the old gold rush town, its unique vertical weathered siding in perfect harmony with the remains of the community as it was before the restoration.

Photo on following page

About twenty-five years had passed since I first hiked up the Cariboo Road, when I returned to reinforce the early memories. The location of the road had changed considerably where the erratic ramblings of the original builders had been straightened, and the washboard had disappeared under paving. Some of the roadside landmarks were no longer to be seen by the highway traveler but could be found by turning off and following the ancient narrow track. The large wooden trestles of the P.G.E. which were once one of the sights of the Cariboo had been replaced with concrete and steel. Travelers who wished to inspect the tremendous gash in the plateau known as The Chasm could still reach it by detouring a few miles on the old road which skirted the edge of the gorge. One of the most prominent of the old

In the little village of Toosey, near Riske Creek, 1965. Toosey Village lies in a hollow of the grassy open hills of the Chilcotin cattle country west of Williams Lake.

Old church at Springhouse, a ranching community south of Williams Lake on the Alkali Lake Road.

landmarks, the church of Bonaparte village, still maintained its roadside position a few miles north of Cache Creek and opposite to it an ornamental gateway marked the entrance to the large native cemetery in which we came upon the headstone of one individual born in the eighteenth century.

Bonaparte Village near Cache Creek, 1958. Detail of entrance to the large and interesting burial ground of the village.

The Clinton Hotel, one of the oldest in the interior, still stood by the roadside at the upper end of town, a durable relic that had seen all the gold rush traffic stream past its doors. It had changed somewhat in appearance since the freighting days, judging by old photographs, one of which, taken in the sixties, shows the building with a large ox team hitched to two covered wagons stopped in front of it. The hotel was destroyed by fire in 1958 a few years short of the century mark.

Old Cariboo Road stopping place, the Clinton Hotel, 1956. For almost a century the Clinton Hotel accommodated travellers on the Cariboo road until it burned in 1958.

This Cariboo trip, which eventually took us to Barkerville, added some interesting landmark photographs to our collection but subjects had diminished during the passage of the years and I regretted the lost opportunities of my younger days. The landscape itself was unchanged but much of it has a monotonous aspect. The level, timbered terrain occupies a great deal of the plateau and is generally unrelieved by any contrasting feature. There are exceptions, of which The Chasm is the most notable, but it is so vast that I have never been able to secure a photograph to do it justice; and the two knobs Lone Butte and Mt. Begbie, would hardly warrant a name in any other part of the province. In this timbered, boulder-strewn country it is a relief to encounter a small lake or isolated ranch, but both east and west of the road side tracks lead to more interesting scenes.

Reminders of the gold rush were naturally scarce and outnumbered by relics of the Cariboo's ranching history. Cottonwood House, on the road in to Barkerville, a few decaying buildings marking the site of Stanley and the sad remains of Barkerville itself including the cemetery almost repossessed by the spruce forest, made but a small collection of remnants of the stirring period that initiated the settlement of interior British Columbia. Barkerville before the restoration was a ragged cluster of buildings, the best preserved of which, St. Saviour's church, exhibited a weathered exterior of vertical boards very much in

At the forks of the road, Pavilion Church, 1973. The old village church on Pavilion Mountain on the route of the original Cariboo Road which was built from Lillooet to Clinton in 1861.

Barkerville, 1957. The spruce forest has grown up in Barkerville since the eighteen-sixties when old photographs showed the site practically denuded of timber. Many of the head boards in the cemetery mark the graves of young men.

harmony with the surroundings. In the half-light of the neglected cemetery, under the trees which had grown up in the graves, still legible inscriptions told of young lives suddenly cut off, and aliens from distant countries come to share the riches of Williams Creek.

Many times, after this trip to Barkerville, we returned to the Cariboo country to explore the web of side roads that seemed to wander haphazard over the plateau, but led us eventually to remote ranches in untamed country. The canyon country west of the road was a perpetual attraction. It seemed the old-time flavor of the Cariboo persisted there when it was no longer to be detected on the highway. Driving west from Clinton the rush of traffic is left behind and the region of the big ranches lies ahead. Various tracks, still pretty much in their primitive state, open the way to Pavilion Mountain, Canoe Creek, Empire Valley, Gang Ranch, Dog Creek and Alkali Lake, all old-time ranch sites dating from years of the gold rush.

Barn near Williams Lake, 1965. Built of logs with a huge loft for hay this type of barn is no longer being built as modern baled hay is generally stacked in the open.

*Grave houses, Anahim Lake, A native burial ground in the back
Chilcotin Country.*

Farther north the Cariboo's most prominent landmark, the Chilcotin Bridge, spans the Fraser in a graceful arch. The locality is west of Williams Lake where a crossing of the canyon was established in 1904 to open the way to the Chilcotin country. The original bridge was a suspension structure set on tall masonry piers with a maze of timber work supporting the approaches on the west bank. It looked a flimsy contraption for such a crossing and was actually not considered equal to the strain put on it by a herd of cattle; only small bunches were permitted to cross at a time. To the beef drives coming out of the Chilcotin to Williams Lake it was a bottleneck that kept the cow-punchers busy for hours, crossing a few head at a time, and very slowly moving the herd from one bank to the other. This was the process when I first knew the Cariboo in the late nineteen-twenties, but by the fifties most of the beef drives were over and the cattle were being transported by the truck load which the old bridge would accept without serious complaint.

The church of Anahim native village occupies high ground in the wide valley.

The old Chimney Creek Bridge over Fraser to the Chilcotin country, west of Williams Lake 1960. A Cariboo landmark since 1904 and one time bottleneck to the beef drives that came into Williams Lake from the Chilcotin ranches. Now replaced by new steel span.

Photo on following page ———→

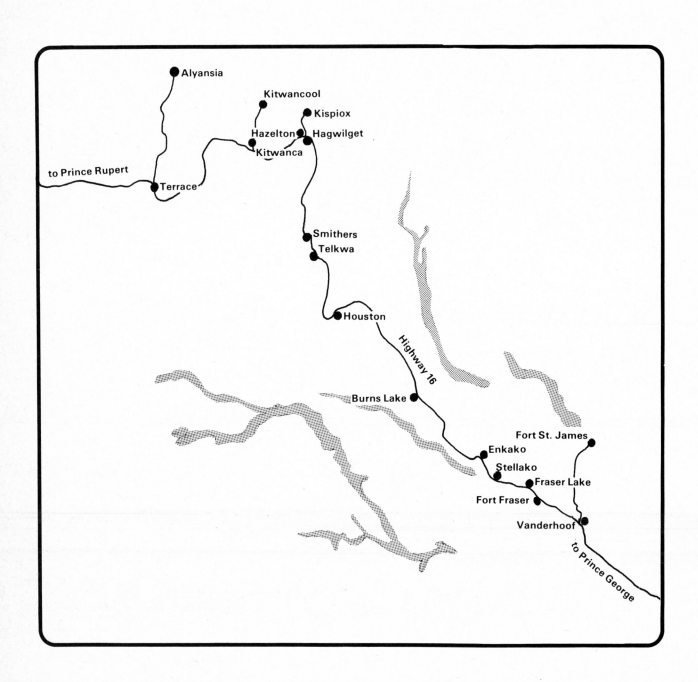

Alyansia

Kitwancool

Kispiox

Hazelton · Hagwilget

Kitwanca

to Prince Rupert

Terrace

Smithers

Telkwa

Houston

Highway 16

Burns Lake

Fort St. James

Enkako

Stellako

Fraser Lake

Fort Fraser

Vanderhoof

to Prince George

West to Skeena.

After many trips to Cariboo and Chilcotin the urge to go farther afield led us to Prince George and the westward route of highway 16. In 1962 long stretches of this road were still unimproved, which made for more interesting traveling, we thought, and certainly gave us time to absorb the fresh scenes that unfolded as we advanced. The center of the province had a more spacious aspect than our own narrow valleys of the south which we had been used to for most of our lives. Even the Cariboo Plateau seemed small compared with the country we were now traveling. Although the terrain was densely forested, small eminences here and there permitted distant views which showed the trees stretching away, endlessly it seemed, to a faint horizon.

Our 1884 map of the province designates this large area variously as "low country," "wide undulating forest country" and farther west, "rounded hills and ridges." It shows a trail from Fort George to Hazelton following pretty much the same route as the present highway, and the nomenclature of the region had at that time been established. In 1910 the English traveler, F.A. Talbot, covered the route by saddle and pack horse in the wake of the Grand Trunk Pacific survey of the line between Fort George and Prince Rupert, and was so impressed by the agricultural possibilities of the region that he entitled his book about the country *The New Garden of Canada*. By the time of our first visit landclearing equipment had advanced to the stage where standing bush could be winrowed entirely by machinery, and the farms and ranches along the route gave evidence of rapid expansion in level fields recently cleared.

In Hazelton cemetery, 1964. Stone grave figures mark native burials in old Hazelton's overgrown cemetery.

Fort Fraser, St. Mary's Anglican. A roadside church on Highway 16.

Endako Anglican church has the bell hung outside the building, 1960.

The fur traders had known it since the beginning of the nineteenth century, but it seemed younger country than Cariboo. There was only spotty settlement before 1910 and there was no road westward to encourage settlers, so the present farms and ranches along the way lack that antique look which is so general with the establishments along the route of the old Cariboo Road. But the country is not without its antiques. Most remarkable of these, and surely the outstanding landmark, is the native church at Fort St. James which is a side trip off the highway from Vanderhoof. Certainly it has the tallest and slenderest spire of any native church I have seen. Our Lady of Good Hope stands on an eroded bank close to the shore of Stuart Lake, a monument to the missionary Father Le-Jacques and the native people who built it in 1873.

Our Lady of Good Hope Catholic Church, Fort St. James, 1968. Standing perilously close to the eroded bank of Stuart Lake this fine church was built by the missionary father LeJacques and the native people in 1873.

Stellaquo native church on Highway 16 near Fraser Lake, 1964.

Although all were overtopped by the lofty spire at Fort St. James, the lesser edifices along the route of Highway 16 showed many variations of great interest. All were worthy of a stop, and some were quite outstanding as some particular light or happy placement in the landscape rendered them the most conspicuous objects in the neighborhood. The little communities along the way, Vanderhoof, Fort Fraser, Nautley, Stellaquo, Endako, Burns Lake, Houston, Telkwa and Moricetown are well-supplied with churches, and westward still the Skeena villages in their beautiful mountain setting display their sacred buildings to unusual advantage. Kispiox, Hagwilget, Gitsegukla, Kitwanga and Kitwancool sit in a valley of rushing creeks and rivers contained but not confined by glorious mountain massifs.

The Skeena and more northerly Nass valleys are remarkable as the only inland locations in British Columbia where the craft of totem carving was practiced and the villages mentioned still contain specimens, standing, fallen or restored, of poles and grave ornaments that were carved long ago. It has been said that these inland totems have been preserved longer than their coast counterparts owing to a drier climate which has given the huge cedar poles a longer standing life. On our first visit in 1962 the Skeena villages had many standing poles, although some were leaning and ready to fall, but early travelers on the Skeena describe the villages as fairly bristling with them. Of these villages Kitwancool had the most interesting and best-preserved collection but much of the site and the adjacent old burial ground was littered with fragments of fallen and decayed poles. Hands, feet and faces from dismembered carvings rested among the weeds and decaying grave houses on the flat below the village.

At old Aiyansh, Nass River, 1963.

Grave figure, Kitwancool, 1964. The big wooden bear that sits in the old burial ground on a flat below the village among many relics of carved poles and decaying grave houses.

Grave houses, Kitwancool, 1964. A native village a dozen miles off Highway 16 between Hazelton and Terrace in Skeena Valley. The custom of totem pole carving spread inland from the coast to the Skeena villages where a number of specimens still stand.

The Nass villages, once noted for their fine totems, now cannot show a single specimen. Until recent years they were beyond the reach of the motorist who lacked a road connection from Highway 16. Eventually a newly-built logging road opened the way from Terrace, sixty miles distant, but still left the villages isolated on the wrong side of the river, a condition that preserved the seclusion of that extraordinary landmark, St. Peter's Anglican Church of Aiyansh. I learned from an informant that the original site of the village was some miles downstream but after a disastrous flood in 1917 it was decided to move the settlement and re-establish it on higher ground. The large church had to be left behind but over the years it was dismantled, transported and rebuilt in the new village where it was finally consecrated in 1962. But several years later the villagers moved again, establishing a new Aiyansh on the opposite side of the river where it had road connection with Terrace. Once more St. Peter's is left behind to brood over a deserted village now sadly reduced by a recent fire.

St. Peters Anglican, old Aiyansh, Nass River, 1963. This fine church occupied a former village site some distance down stream but the village was abandoned after a disastrous flood. St. Peters was dismantled and rebuilt on its present site but is now once more left behind as the villagers have migrated across the river.

Community Hall in the large native village of Kispiox near Hazelton on Highway 16. This village is also noted for its totem poles, some of which have been recently restored.

We made several trips to the Skeena, regretting the neglect of previous years. Once we came in spring and followed the vigorous river down to the estuary, marvelling at the enormous trees washed out by the freshet and stranded along the shoreline. The mountains were loaded with masses of immaculate snow and the creeks had hardly commenced to cascade down their precipitous sides. The ferrymen told us the river was abnormally low after a backward spring; they feared a sudden rise when the warm weather came. It came, and the river went wild, washing out road and railroad. But the valley was beautiful with the tender green of leafing aspens and the massed white blossoms of saskatoon. Brilliant snow peaks hovered high over every scene. We wandered through the villages, admiring the weathered figures of the totems posed against the mountain background. Kitwanga still possessed a row of poles along the main street but many others lay where they had fallen in the grass. At Kitwancool we came upon a large wooden figure of a bear in the old burial ground below the village. Was it the same bear that Emily Carr encountered when she painted in the village many years ago? In her book **Klee Wyck** she relates how, when driven from her easel by a heavy rain storm, she was startled by coming upon the bear suddenly while beating down the nettles by a grave house to which she was fleeing for shelter.

Church at Kitwancool, Skeena Valley, with bell tower, 1962.

Photo on following page ⟶

In Hazelton, old time river port on Skeena River off Highway 16, Prince George to Prince Rupert. There are many interesting graves with the fancy decorations in vogue 70 to 80 years ago. The cemetery is now much overgrown.

Catholic Church at Smithers, 1963.

Bell tower and church at Kitwanga, Skeena Valley, 1962. Kitwanga, a native village noted for its totem poles which used to border the main street back from the river bank but have now mostly fallen. On Highway 16 between Hazelton and Terrace.

We spent some time in the cemetery of old Hazelton, finding many fascinating relics in wood and stone and were sad to see that vandals had accomplished what nature had failed to achieve - some of the stone grave figures had been overturned and broken. Thus the fancied imperishable stone had failed to outlast the elaborate wooden ornaments that were so popular in former times. The brush was growing wild in this old cemetery, and some of the grave enclosures were scattered in fragments over the site.

In contrast the well-maintained church in nearby Hagwilget, poised on a high knoll above the village, made a more enduring landmark. It is the most handsome of all the Skeena churches and quite the most prominent. Surely no better site could have been chosen!

In the little settlement of Hagensborg in Bella Coola Valley, 1965. It is on the route of Alexander Mackenzie's famous journey of 1793 to the Pacific Coast.

Reluctantly we turned homeward from this spring journey. It was the second of our trips to the Skeena and we never afterwards found the valley in quite the same mood. Subsequent visits were made with more comfort but less sense of adventure. Highway improvements were constantly robbing us of washboard and dust, and the sudden sharp corners that revealed only at the last moment some fresh and exquisite scene. I remember how high the mountains seemed through gaps in the trees along the old crooked roads. The modern highway spreads an empty foreground of paving in front of every passing view. It by-passes the old landmarks and introduces new ones of a totally different character. Fortunately there are many side roads that offer a temporary escape from too much civilization and we took these whenever possible. On these quiet country tracks we could live leisurely the life we have loved and perhaps for a while delude ourselves that all the highlights of our younger days had not completely passed away.